Compost Gold

by Nancy Furstinger
illustrated by Gail Piazza

Scott Foresman
is an imprint of

PEARSON

Glenview, Illinois • Boston, Massachusetts • Mesa, Arizona
Shoreview, Minnesota • Upper Saddle River, New Jersey

Illustrations
Gail Piazza

Photographs
Every effort has been made to secure permission and provide appropriate credit for photographic material. The publisher deeply regrets any omission and pledges to correct errors called to its attention in subsequent editions.

Unless otherwise acknowledged, all photographs are the property of Pearson Education, Inc.

Photo locators denoted as follows: Top (T), Center (C), Bottom (B), Left (L), Right (R), Background (Bkgd).

4 (CL) ©Jim Craigmyle/Corbis, (BC) ©Design Pics Inc./Alamy, (CR) ©Peter Hendrie/Getty Images; 6 ©ullstein-Hechtenberg/Peter Arnold, Inc.

ISBN 13: 978-0-328-39394-7
ISBN 10:   0-328-39394-0

Copyright © Pearson Education, Inc. or its affiliate(s). All Rights Reserved.
Printed in the United States of America. This publication is protected by copyright and permission should be obtained from the publisher prior to any prohibited reproduction, storage in a retrieval system, or transmission in any form or by any means, electronic, mechanical, photocopying, recording, or otherwise. For information regarding permission(s), write to: Pearson School Rights and Permissions, One Lake Street, Upper Saddle River, New Jersey 07458.

Pearson and Scott Foresman are trademarks, in the U.S. and/or other countries, of Pearson Education, Inc. or its affiliate(s).

1 2 3 4 5 6 7 8 9 10 V010 17 16 15 14 13 12 11 10 09 08

Rosa grows roses in her garden. Her roses are so pretty that all of her neighbors want to buy them. Joe grows giant pumpkins in his garden. His pumpkins have won prizes.

Both Rosa and Joe are very good at gardening. Both also have a secret to growing such healthy plants—they add **compost** to the soil in their gardens.

Last week, Ms. Snow, their teacher, asked the students to find a partner and choose a topic to learn about for science class. Rosa and Joe got together to learn more about compost.

What is Compost?

Rosa and Joe already know some things about compost because they use it in their gardens. They wanted to know more, so they read about compost at the library.

Compost has been around for a very long time. It has been around for as long as there have been plants. When plants die, they slowly break down. These dead plants **transform** into a dark brown material. This is compost, and it creates food for plants. Compost is found around the world in forests, grasslands, and jungles.

forest

grassland

jungle

Why Compost?

Why would people want to make their own compost? Rosa and Joe knew the answer to that question. They wanted to share the facts with their class.

Compost makes the soil better for growing plants, and it can help plants grow to be stronger. Compost can also help keep plants from getting sick. And it can help stop bugs from hurting the plants.

Compost can do all of these good things without adding bad things to the soil. Compost does not cost a lot of money, and it is easy to make.

without compost   **with compost**

Rosa and Joe made another important **discovery** about compost. Every day, yard and kitchen wastes get thrown away. These wastes take up space in landfills. A landfill is a place where waste and garbage are buried. Landfills are a growing problem in many places.

Compost can help fix this problem. Instead of tossing out wastes, gardeners can use them to grow plants! They can **recycle** wastes into compost.

What You Can Compost

Many things can be put in a compost pile instead of in the garbage can. Rosa and Joe made a poster showing what their class can use to make compost.

People can make compost from dead leaves, grass clippings, and twigs. If they live on a farm, they can add hay and straw.

They can also use many kitchen wastes. Eggshells, nutshells, fruits, and vegetables can all be added to a compost pile. People can also add pieces of cardboard, newspapers, and paper towels to the compost.

What You Can Compost

- leaves
- grass clippings
- twigs
- hay
- straw
- eggshells
- nut shells
- old fruits and vegetables
- cardboard
- newspapers
- paper towels

What You Cannot Compost

Rosa and Joe made another poster to show that some wastes should not go into the compost pile. They should go into the garbage instead, because these wastes might make the compost smell bad. They also might invite flies and others animals to come around.

Meat, fish, and bones should not be added to compost, nor should cheese and milk be added. Things that are not natural shouldn't be added to compost either.

Start Your Pile of Compost

Rosa and Joe know the best way to start a compost pile. First they need to find an open dry, shady spot. The best compost is formed in **layers**.

Rosa and Joe start off with a layer of brown waste. The brown waste layer can be made up of leaves and broken branches.

Now they are ready to add the next layer. They put a layer of green waste on top of the brown waste. The green layer can be made of grass clippings and old fruits and vegetables.

green waste

brown waste

Next, Rosa puts soil on top of the two layers. Then she mixes all three layers together, using a rake and a shovel. After she finishes mixing, she adds another layer of brown waste.

Now Joe adds water. He uses a hose to spray the mixed compost. Then he covers the compost pile to keep the water in.

Over the next few weeks, Rosa and Joe's families add waste to the compost pile. They add the waste in layers. Rosa and Joe make sure to mix the compost layers often.

Rosa and Joe take good care of their compost pile. It doesn't smell or attract flies or other animals. Their compost pile quickly grows to be five feet tall!

Compost Inside

Rosa and Joe want to tell students who live in apartments how they can make compost inside their homes. They can use food scraps to make the compost, which can be used for a rooftop garden or even for window boxes.

Rosa and Joe learn that you can use a garbage can to make kitchen compost. First, find a garbage can that fits in a cabinet **underneath** a sink. Then punch holes in the bottom of the garbage can and set it on a waterproof tray. Next, fill half the can with peat moss. Peat moss is natural and is made of plants. Then add just enough water to make the peat moss wet. Then add the right food scraps.

Finally, add red worms to the garbage can. People can buy these worms from a worm farm. Red worms are known as compost worms. Every week, each worm can have about 12 baby worms.

The worms eat fruit and vegetable scraps. Rosa and Joe wonder how many worms it would take to eat all the kitchen scraps. They learn that in one week, 2,000 worms can eat about one pound of food scraps!

Compost for All Seasons

Rosa and Joe also learn that they can make compost outdoors during all seasons.

Spring is the best time to start a compost pile. After the grass is first mowed, clippings can be added to a layer of old leaves. In the summer, more grass clippings and other plants can be added to the pile. In the fall, dead leaves on top can help the pile grow. The pile grows the slowest in the winter.

spring

fall

In one or two months, the compost at the bottom of the pile will turn a dark color. This change in color shows that the compost is now ready to use.

Rosa and Joe add a layer of compost to their gardens. They use a rake or shovel to mix the compost into the soil.

Compost Tea

Rosa and Joe also learned about compost tea. It is not a tea to drink! Compost tea feeds plants.

After their compost is ready, Rosa and Joe fill a large bucket halfway with compost. They fill the rest of the bucket with water. They leave the compost in the water for several days. Then they pour it through a screen, which lets only the water pass through. The water they have is compost tea. Rosa and Joe use this mixture to water their plants. It makes the soil healthy and helps their plants to grow.

Rosa and Joe are ready to tell the class about compost. They take turns telling about each stage of making compost. They also show many pictures of compost piles.

Rosa brings in a picture of her roses. Joe shows off his biggest pumpkin. Rosa and Joe decide to help others in their neighborhood start their own compost piles.

Now Try This

Fact Cards for Compost

This book has a lot of information about compost. It can be hard to remember it all. You can make a card game using the facts from this book. This will help you remember all the fun facts about compost piles.

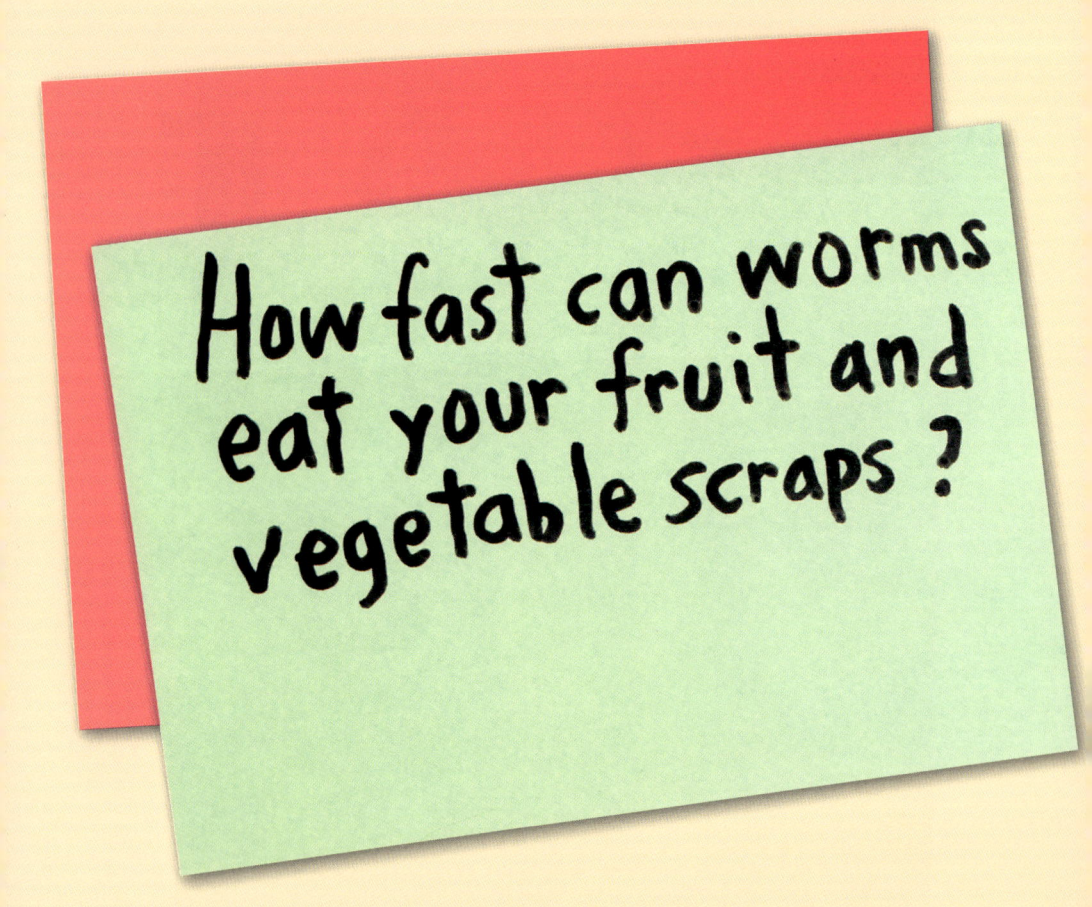

How fast can worms eat your fruit and vegetable scraps?

Here's How To Do It!

1. Use the information you learned about compost to make five fact cards.

2. On one side of an index card, write a question about compost from the book.

3. On the other side of the card, write a fact that answers the question. Then draw a picture that illustrates the answer.

4. Trade fact cards with a partner. Try to answer each question. Look on the other side of the card to see if your answer is correct.

In one week, 2,000 worms can eat one pound.

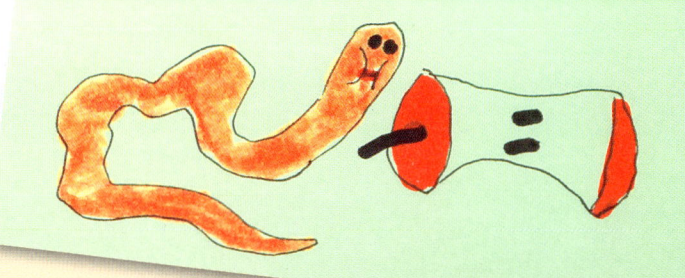

Glossary

compost *n.* a mixture of leaves, grass, and other natural things that help plants grow

discovery *n.* something found out

layer *n.* a thickness of something

recycle *v.* to treat something so it can be used again

transform *v.* to change the form or appearance of something

underneath *prep.* below or under